Time Management

A Comprehensive Manual For Unleashing Your Maximum Potential Via Optimal Time Management Approaches, Comprising Valuable Insights

(Strategies And Methods For Enhancing Productivity)

Sławomir Czapiewski

TABLE OF CONTENT

Goal Setting 1

How To Overcome Procrastination 11

Creating A Schedule 19

Key Tenets To Be Mindful Of In Time Management 24

Procrastination 40

Strategies For Establishing Goals That Are Both Effective And Attainable 51

Dealing With Distractions 87

Time Management Skills 105

Displaying The Appropriate Attitude And Mindset 114

Intentional Time Management Solution 131

Factors Contributing To Ineffective Time Management 140

Methods To Prevent Overexertion 142

Goal Setting

"Individuals who possess clear objectives tend to achieve success, as they possess a clear sense of direction.

Earl Nightingale

Goal setting and time management are intrinsically linked - they are both indispensable and paramount components that must be implemented in order to establish and attain short-term and long-term objectives. This commonality exists between small business owners and managers of established businesses, as both groups must establish goals in order to guarantee the achievement of their milestones.

It is widely acknowledged that individuals who establish goals tend to achieve greater success. Through the establishment of attainable short-term objectives and actionable tasks, you significantly enhance your progress towards the desired outcome and ultimate achievements.

In the realm of business, it is imperative that the compilation of objectives transcends a mere enumeration; rather, they ought to be unambiguous to all members of the workforce, encompass a well-structured strategy, and be harmonious with both the company's yearly targets and broader overarching goals. The rationales behind the significance and advantages of establishing strategic, quarterly objectives for your company's productivity and success are as follows:

- The establishment of quarterly objectives promotes accountability and enhances employee performance: it is expected that every individual within the organization will be equipped with a set of achievable goals, accompanied by a well-defined action plan that facilitates the achievement of each goal. Implementing quarterly objectives aids in task prioritization for employees throughout the year and provides managers with a means to monitor team progress. Additionally, it provides managers with enhanced insight into the performance and productivity of each individual employee. Establishing attainable short-term objectives contributes to the progress of employees' career advancement. By implementing quarterly incentives or merit-based initiatives, individuals are inclined to enhance their performance by setting and accomplishing these goals, thereby increasing their motivation. Recognizing employees who consistently achieve their objectives, inspire ongoing goal-setting, and foster a culture that values internal recognition of accomplishments. Consequently, this will enhance employee contentment and foster greater company allegiance.

Implementing quarterly objectives guarantees the ongoing relevance of metrics, as successful businesses necessitate an understanding of how these metrics are aligned with the overarching goals of the company. While the enduring nature of long-term goals may necessitate minimal alteration over the course of the company's lifespan, it is probable that short-term objectives will necessitate periodic reassessment to accommodate the growth and evolution of the business. Conducting a thorough evaluation of your metrics in the form of quarterly objectives will guarantee that your organization maintains the ability to gauge the effectiveness of current strategies and identify areas requiring adaptations. Additionally, your team will have the opportunity to utilize any newly acquired data to adapt and revise their objectives accordingly, instilling a sense of assurance in their ongoing accomplishments aligned with the organization's overarching vision.

- The establishment of quarterly objectives facilitates the preservation of sustainable progress: attaining these quarterly objectives poses a formidable challenge for any enterprise. Implementing quarterly objectives guarantees the company's unwavering attention towards mitigating challenges, thereby precluding any potential setbacks. These objectives may encompass the achievement of acquiring additional clientele on a monthly basis. Please be informed that attaining a stable pattern of growth poses a significant challenge for every business entity. Establishing short-term goals helps to ensure that the leadership of the company maintains a focused approach, enabling the establishment of essential processes during the initial stages of success. This proactive approach diminishes the likelihood of encountering challenges related to growth in the future.

- Quarterly objectives aid in visualizing the overarching vision: all goals, whether short or long-term, ought to be formulated while keeping the broader perspective in consideration. Establishing quarterly objectives fosters a sense of achievability for not only the managerial cadre, but also for all employees entrusted with the responsibility of fulfilling growth-oriented endeavors. Employees are more inclined to attain success when they possess a comprehensive comprehension of their designated responsibilities and how their individual objectives synergistically contribute towards the accomplishment of their organization, aligning with the broader scope of the company.

For certain individuals, establishing objectives may appear straightforward – you simply document a few significant accomplishments, diligently engage in pursuing them, and voila, the triumph you have perpetually sought is realized...

Or not.

The issue at hand pertains to the fact that a majority of individuals encounter difficulties in their endeavors to accomplish their goals, as they lack the requisite knowledge on translating a goal into a feasible and manageable plan on a daily basis. They lack proficiency in the art of transforming objectives into consistent behaviors. The key is to formulate a strategic course of action and adhere to it unwaveringly, placing paramount importance on wholeheartedly dedicating oneself to its implementation. Utilizing the technique of SMART goal setting can provide assistance in addressing that matter.

SMART represents an initialism denoting the key attributes of Specific, Measurable, Achievable, Relevant, and Time-Based. Every component within the SMART framework collaborates to generate a goal that is meticulously designed, unambiguous, and can be easily monitored.

S Specific: Articulate your objectives with utmost precision and conciseness, leaving no room for ambiguity in delineating what you intend to accomplish. The further you refine and specify your objective, the greater your comprehension of the requisite measures for its attainment will become.

Example: My objective is to secure a role as a Senior Management Assistant within a prominent legal establishment.

Measurable: What empirical evidence can substantiate your progression towards achieving your objective? If your objective was to secure the position of Senior M.A., you could gauge your progress by assessing the number of times you have submitted applications and the frequency with which you receive invitations to interviews. Establishing these key objectives will afford you the chance to reassess and rectify, if necessary. Ensure that you grant yourself a reward upon successfully reaching any significant milestones.

Is the goal you have established feasible? Establishing attainable objectives within a predetermined time frame will effectively sustain your motivation and concentration. Prior to embarking on the pursuit of a goal, it is imperative to ascertain if it is presently attainable or if there are any supplementary measures that must be undertaken to enhance one's preparedness.

Relevance: When establishing personal objectives, it is essential to assess their pertinence. Every one of your objectives ought to be in congruence with your values and broader, future objectives. If a goal fails to align with your overarching aspirations, it may warrant reconsideration.

How To Overcome Procrastination

It has been widely acknowledged that procrastination is a detrimental factor that compromises the effective utilization of time. Your capacity to conquer procrastination and adhere to a predetermined schedule can serve as a decisive determinant between achieving success or experiencing failure.

Nevertheless, the reality remains that procrastination is a universal phenomenon. Everyone is burdened with excessive tasks and an inadequate amount of time. However, if each individual engages in the act of delaying or postponing tasks, what distinguishes the high achiever from the low achiever?

Simple. The accomplished individual tends to delay the completion of tasks and activities that hold little or no significance.

The underperforming individual engages in procrastination when it comes to completing tasks of significant importance. In order to achieve peak performance, it is imperative that you commit to practicing 'strategic delay' moving forward.

Make a deliberate and conscious decision regarding the tasks that you plan to postpone. Please examine your schedule for the day and prioritize tasks that you will delay until after completing more crucial ones. One should engage in conscientious and deliberate effort rather than engaging in accidental and automatic procrastination.

We frequently exhibit a tendency to postpone our most significant responsibilities, which often coincide with our most valuable tasks. There exists a range of strategies that can be employed to effectively combat or at the very least, effectively address, procrastination. In fact, there are libraries full of books, on the subject of overcoming procrastination.

Herein lie several commendable propositions that can be promptly initiated.

Mental Programming

"Do it now!"

These words may be considered as the most potent means to enhance one's productivity. Anytime you catch yourself delaying the completion of a significant undertaking, recite the phrase "Execute it immediately! Execute it immediately! Execute it immediately!" with fervor and excitement.

The remarkable phenomenon is that, following the repetition of these words ad infinitum, an individual will inevitably and subconsciously feel compelled to remain focused on their utmost significant undertaking and accomplish that responsibility prior to engaging in any other activities.

Completing Larger Tasks

Henry Ford once wrote, "Any goal can be achieved if you break it down into enough small parts."

Any significant endeavor that you are required to fulfill can be accomplished with greater ease by breaking it down into sufficiently smaller components - thus dividing your task into manageable increments.

Take a piece of paper and write down every small part of the task that you have to do, in sequence, from the first little job to the final job that completes the task. Afterwards, exercise self-control to prioritize the first item on your list.

Occasionally, opting to initiate the first phase of a substantial undertaking can facilitate the execution of subsequent stages, thereby streamlining the progression of each subsequent step. Initiating a significant undertaking will facilitate the cultivation of the necessary drive and enthusiasm to persistently labor until the assignment is fully achieved.

The technique known as the Salami Slice Method

A modification of the "bite-sized pieces" approach to overcoming procrastination is referred to as the "salami slice method." Much like how one would not attempt to consume an entire loaf of salami in a single bite, one does not endeavor to complete a sizable task in one time period.

Instead, the task is approached through a method of salami slicing, which involves systematically reducing the size of the task by incrementally slicing off small portions. You subsequently decide to accomplish that particular element before proceeding to another task.

Each instance you commence work on your primary assignment, particularly in instances where you are faced with an abundance of additional urgent obligations, make a commitment to sequentially accomplish individual components of the task. Frequently, this approach will initiate your progress on the project and facilitate the subsequent completion of subsequent phases such as two, three, four, and so forth.

Cultivate a Perception of Immediacy

A sense of urgency is a profoundly exceptional and highly prized human attribute within the realm of professional endeavors. It has been approximated that a mere 2% of individuals demonstrate expedience in accomplishing tasks.

In a survey conducted among 300 executives, it was found that 85% of CEOs offered a unanimous response when asked about the actions employees could take to advance their careers within their respective corporations. The qualities that held the utmost significance in their evaluation were:

The capacity to establish priorities, and

The capacity to initiate the crucial task and accomplish it expeditiously and proficiently.

When one acquires a track record of initiating their most crucial tasks and accomplishing them efficiently and skillfully, they will be astounded by the multitude of prospects that can arise.

Creating A Schedule

Having familiarized yourself with steps one through four, it is now appropriate to synthesize these steps into a comprehensive timetable.

If one has a multitude of tasks to accomplish within a given day, it would be prudent to establish a schedule. A standard schedule will encompass the following aspects, all of which constitute integral components of your daily workload.

Midday break - Utilize this opportunity to step away from the corporate setting for some rejuvenating outdoor activities and physical exertion. Consume a balanced diet and refrain from hastily devouring your meal.

2 – 4 – Regularly scheduled meetings, record keeping, and telephone correspondence

4 – 5 - Organizing and tidying the remaining items on your desk in preparation for tomorrow.

Indeed, that is a rather broad summary. Nonetheless, it is worth noting that there will be areas characterized by considerable concentration as well as areas with relatively lower concentration, affording you the opportunity to take a respite during lunchtime. It is advisable to incorporate a short break for refreshment at the mid-morning and mid-afternoon intervals. I will elucidate the significance of engaging in periodic rest intervals, as they have been shown to enhance productivity instead of diminishing it.

It is imperative that you incorporate all of your daily objectives into your schedule. The schedule enables individuals to establish a time restriction for each task, thereby fostering heightened mindfulness regarding the progression of time. If necessary, you may make slight adjustments to these parameters throughout the day without any issue. It is crucial to establish a certain level of organization to your daily routine to ensure that you are aware of any backlog and can effectively utilize designated periods for less demanding tasks in order to make up for lost time. The objective is to complete the aforementioned list within the designated time frame, as there is no better source of motivation than crossing off the items on your agenda that have indeed been accomplished. Please ensure that you are equipped with a marker and capable of performing the task at hand, as it is a crucial component of the ritual that ensures your progress remains on track.

It is imperative to allocate a specific duration throughout the day to engage in communication and collaboration with individuals. This is an integral component of your professional itinerary. Throughout the forthcoming chapters, you will delve into the reasons behind the significance of this matter. In striving to surpass your competitors, it is equally imperative to cultivate support from others, necessitating the granting of opportunities to aid them in attaining their respective objectives. Engaging in this type of managerial responsibility on a regular basis and demonstrating your ability to provide assistance to others also positions you favorably for potential advancement within the organization.

Call to Action

Acquire a piece of paper and proceed to compose a schedule tailored to your personal needs. This schedule should encompass all the hours during which you are active and should encompass the entirety of all feasible tasks. Please affix this schedule to your wall and make a point to regularly consult it to keep track of the tasks that require your attention.

Key Tenets To Be Mindful Of In Time Management

In relation to employment and devising a productive schedule to adhere to, Emma Donaldson-Feilder, a psychologist, provides several recommendations. First and foremost, ascertain your life objectives, contemplate the person you aspire to become, and determine the accomplishments you aim to achieve in your existence. To master time management we must first decide our life direction and once this is decided we ought to use it as if it were a principle. This is due to the fact that having a clear understanding of one's ultimate life objectives and long-term vision facilitates the systematic pursuit of intermediary objectives at smaller and medium scales. Having a clear understanding of your objectives will provide you with more insight into effectively organizing your day, enhancing personal growth, and making progress towards your overarching aspirations. Additionally, a recommended course of action would be to create a comprehensive inventory. I am referring to a document in the form of a to-do list or an itemized outline. Every day, compile a concise inventory of all the tasks you aim to accomplish throughout the day. This facilitates organizational efficiency, aids in maintaining focus, and provides a clear measure of your progress. Individuals have the option to create numerous lists should they wish to categorize tasks based on their level of importance, urgency, or according to high, medium, and low priority. Alternatively, one may choose to arrange tasks in accordance with their relative significance and level of immediacy. I have personally embraced Emma Donaldson-Fielder's methodology of maintaining a singular daily list to avoid any potential confusion. This approach enables me to efficiently manage my time, streamline complexities, and, most significantly, consolidate everything in a singular location to monitor my progress accurately. It is important to ensure the accessibility of your to-do list. If you prefer not to use the traditional pen and paper method, consider maintaining a digital record on your personal mobile device. One can effortlessly accomplish this task by acquiring a complimentary note-taking application, provided they do not already possess one. By engaging in this practice, you will promptly gain entry to your assigned tasks and objectives for the day. I have a personal inclination towards jotting down my thoughts on paper. I habitually keep a notebook within close proximity at all times, finding this method more convenient than the process of accessing a laptop, opening specific files, and creating or modifying a to-do list. Once inscribed onto physical documentation, any modifications are irrevocable, rendering the information permanent.

Step 4: Set Priorities

In order to discern your priorities, it is necessary to ascertain which matters are of significance and which require immediate attention. "All activities can be categorized into four quadrants, which include:

1. Crucial and Significant: Crucial and significant activities refer to tasks or assignments that require immediate attention or prompt completion. Engaging in these activities often induces stress, thus disregarding them and the consequential stress may result in adverse repercussions, such as customer loss, termination of employment, or elevated blood pressure, among others. Attend to these activities or tasks promptly.

2. Non-pressing yet substantial: Items or responsibilities falling within this quadrant can be attended to at a later time, although they hold significance in relation to your personal objectives and aspirations. The allocation of time

towards these activities yields enduring advantages that enhance the quality of your life. A considerable number of individuals have a tendency to disregard these obligations or pursuits under the assumption that they will eventually be attended to. In order to achieve the inherent worth associated with these endeavors, one must strategically allocate cognitive resources and actively invest the necessary amount of time and energy.

Instances of such responsibilities encompass activities such as engaging in physical exercise, undergoing medical examinations, pursuing education, attending yearly general assemblies, and so forth.

3. Pressing yet Insignificant: These activities or tasks require prompt

attention, but are inconsequential in relation to one's overarching objectives. You are expected to engage with these activities or tasks under the assumption that their urgency signifies their importance. For instance, receiving a phone call or message from a friend seeking conversation due to boredom, or successfully completing an elective course requirement are illustrative examples of this.

It is possible to modify the tasks or activities in this quadrant to be categorized as "urgent and important" when they hold significance to an individual of great importance to you.

4. Insignificant and Nonessential: These activities or tasks can be considered as fruitless pursuits, as they lack the requirement for immediate attention

and hold no significance towards your personal objectives. Engaging in these activities or tasks may lead to subsequent feelings of remorse. To mitigate this issue, either eliminate them entirely or reserve their execution until all tasks in the initial three quadrants have been completed. Examples illustrating these activities encompass engaging in interactive electronic entertainment, engaging in the engaging art of storytelling with acquaintances such as friends, colleagues, or fellow students.

Construct a task list aimed at facilitating the assessment and ranking of your assignments.

Strategies for Developing a Productive Task Agenda

Presented below are guidelines to assist you in developing a To-do list that facilitates the optimization of your work productivity:

1. Document all activities/tasks: document all your activities, tasks, obligations, and conflicting engagements for a day or a week.

2. Please outline your main objectives: based on a review of your activities, identify and document your key goals for the day or the week. Your primary objectives encompass the fundamental, immediate targets that must be accomplished on a daily or weekly basis in order to progress towards your overarching, long-term aspirations.

3. Take into account the principle known as the Pareto principle or 80/20 rule: According to this rule, 20% of the tasks

you engage in are of significance and contribute to 80% of your success within a given day or week. Conversely, 80% of the tasks you undertake are of lesser importance and only account for 20% of your overall success within a given day or week. Identify the activities that contribute significantly, up to 20%, towards accomplishing your objectives.

4. Assess the Significance and Time Sensitivity of Activities: Based on your activity log, analyze the activities that hold the highest importance and the potential ramifications of not achieving them.

5. Arrange your activities in order of importance by employing a ranking system, strategically plan and harmonize your engagements, prioritizing those of

utmost significance down to the ones of lesser significance.

6. Eliminate: Elimination involves the removal of activities that are situated at the lower end of your prioritization, namely those that are less probable to be accomplished. Eliminate any activities that fail to contribute towards attaining your objectives and are ultimately time-wasting endeavors; engaging in leisure activities such as playing video games serves as an apt illustration.

Prioritize completing the significant tasks first. By giving precedence to your tasks, you will commence engaging in fruitful endeavors that will progressively propel you towards your predetermined objectives. You will cease experiencing excessive fatigue and a lack of recollection regarding your actions at the conclusion of each day or week.

Subsequently, we will acquire the knowledge of attaining order and structure.

2. Why do we fail to achieve our full potential?

To begin with, it is evident that technology, especially social media, greatly hampers our daily focus and attention. It should be relatively straightforward to deactivate these devices or refrain from acknowledging them. However, for a considerable number of individuals, our fondness for these gadgets outweighs our rationality, leading us to succumb to curiosity whenever a new notification emerges.

Not only does technology hinder our ability to complete tasks, but our ingrained habits also play a role, such as attempting to multitask without proper planning for each individual task. Although multi-tasking can be advantageous, it entails a division of one's attention and focus. Based on a research conducted by Stanford University in 2009, it was observed that humans do not possess the ability to effectively multitask; rather, they exhibit the capability to swiftly shift their focus from one task to another. This implies that our concentration diminishes, thereby potentially compromising our capacity to perform tasks effectively.

To achieve expedited and precise task completion, it is imperative to maintain a high level of concentration. I must acknowledge that accomplishing this is indeed more challenging in practice, and I propose that you consider breaking down each goal into its constituent sub-tasks necessary for its achievement and allocate specific periods of time to each of these sub-tasks. This will aid you in preserving your concentration throughout the execution of these tasks, and the abbreviated yet intensive periods of work will significantly enhance your overall productivity. When engaging in the process of task sub-division, there exist a plethora of efficacious productivity applications which greatly facilitate the organization and monitoring of sub-tasks and objectives. A thorough examination of these applications will be conducted subsequently in this informative resource.

One additional factor contributing to individuals occasionally underperforming in terms of time management is inadequate physical well-being and fitness. This aspect significantly influences energy levels. We will examine this matter with greater elaboration in the subsequent section.

Procrastination

Procrastination can be described as the deliberate avoidance of completing a necessary task. At times, one may encounter a situation wherein pressing obligations are neglected, even though they ought to be promptly addressed. A significant number of individuals tend to delay engaging in certain tasks due to their preference for enjoyable activities, leading them to prioritize those over less enjoyable tasks. In addition, it is often observed that individuals tend to prioritize less pressing responsibilities over their more pressing counterparts. This situation persists until the final moment when the completed tasks are due, at which point one may resort to hurriedly completing the tasks or providing justifications in order to avoid their completion.

Procrastination exerts a significant impact on various aspects of your life. One could possibly engage in delaying the task of tidying the household or attending to various matters pertaining to the household, such as undertaking minor repairs, seeking medical attention, accomplishing an academic assignment, assisting an acquaintance or family member, and so forth. Ultimately, one begins to experience a sense of remorse for having neglected to undertake a task that could have been addressed much earlier. Other individuals experience a sense of inadequacy and perceive themselves as incapable of achieving personal success. Depression may also ensue, particularly if one consistently defers vital commitments in life. One may also begin to experience sentiments of self-doubt, consequently feeling inadequate in all aspects of life.

Why do people procrastinate?

Procrastination poses a significant challenge for individuals who exhibit chronic postponement tendencies, as they struggle to decipher effective strategies for overcoming this behavior. It is not a matter of choice for them, as procrastination would not be contemplated if it were up to them.

Procrastinators endeavor to attain immediate satisfaction, thereby limiting their mental attention to the current moment. They fail to consider the wisdom imparted by past experiences or devote contemplation towards future endeavors, as their primary concern centers around the present and its potential for instant gratification.

For an individual who tends to procrastinate, recreational pursuits regularly occur, even during periods when they ought to be avoided. He is unable to derive any pleasure during that period, as it is accompanied by feelings of guilt, anxiety, and occasionally self-loathing.

By what means does he accomplish his tasks?

The procrastinator harbors an intense fear of panic, which is a singular source of distress. Within the psyche of every individual prone to procrastination lies a dormant sense of panic, which typically awakens when impending deadlines draw near or there exists a potential for peril, public humiliation, or any other form of calamity. For the panic monster to emerge, the resulting repercussions must be significant, prompting procrastinators to strategize methods for accomplishing their tasks during this period.

Why is procrastination bad?

Certain individuals fail to perceive procrastination as an issue, provided that they are ultimately accomplishing their tasks. Nevertheless, there exist numerous aspects pertaining to procrastination that render it detrimental, encompassing the following:

Procrastination is unpleasant

Despite devoting a significant portion of their time to indulging in pleasurable activities, procrastinators are unable to fully experience the gratification and deserved respite that can only be attained by diligently completing tasks within a well-structured timeframe. There persists a prevailing sentiment that a substantial amount of tasks remain, which fails to elicit any sense of enjoyment. Furthermore, there is a distinct absence of contentment when one succumbs to a state of panic, precipitated by the belated recognition that the deadline is imminently upon them.

A procrastinator achieves less

The combination of time pressure and a heightened state of anxiety impede one's ability to perform at an optimal level of effectiveness. Significant accomplishments are unattainable in the presence of persistent procrastination. In the end, you are unable to achieve your full potential. Ultimately, what transpires is a perpetual dissatisfaction with oneself and past achievements. This phenomenon instigates self-antipathy and fosters a sense of inadequacy in comparison to one's peers.

There exist numerous tasks that remain unfinished.

The panic monster only strikes when the deadline for the things that the procrastinator has to do approaches but he does not experience panic when he has to do the things he wants to do in life. This implies that his actions are strictly limited to tasks that are obligatory in nature. Other endeavors encompassing personal development, such as engaging in literary pursuits, frequenting fitness establishments, and partaking in physical activities, do not ultimately culminate in fulfilment. Consequently, you are deprived of the opportunity to engage in valuable pursuits that can enhance your well-being.

What to do

Procrastinators should acquire the ability to accomplish tasks effectively and efficiently, which entails the implementation of a well-devised strategy and the subsequent execution of tasks in accordance with said strategy.

Planning poses minimal challenges, thus rendering it an undertaking that a procrastinator can effortlessly accomplish. It is imperative to engage in meticulous planning that encompasses intricate details and systematic procedures in order to make the task appear attainable, thus eliminating any inclination to procrastinate. Through meticulous and strategic planning, one can confidently anticipate long-term success.

One common cause of procrastination can be attributed to perceiving a task as overly challenging. However, by employing efficient planning techniques, one can unveil the inherent simplicity and ease of completing the task, thereby facilitating an easier commencement.

The act of planning will enable you to discern the most pressing tasks that require immediate completion, allowing you to ascertain the sequential order in which these tasks should be finalized. Once a victor has been identified, commencing the task at hand becomes straightforward. Furthermore, once initiation has taken place, it proves arduous to discontinue until the entirety of the undertaking has reached completion.

A formidable endeavor becomes more approachable and feasible after systematic deconstruction during the planning phase, precisely what a procrastinator requires to initiate the task.

Strategies For Establishing Goals That Are Both Effective And Attainable

You may perceive yourself as a highly motivated individual with clear objectives. Nevertheless, a considerable number of your objectives are not yielding desirable outcomes, leaving you with a pervasive sense of pursuing an unceasing ambition. Although your aspirations may appear commendable initially, upon reflection, you may come to recognize their highly ambitious and arduous nature. There is currently no viable method for you to achieve your goals as they are currently articulated. You have encountered a setback in attaining your goal due to its unattainable nature.

Have you ever pondered upon the principles of effectively establishing achievable objectives, thereby empowering yourself to manifest your aspirations? You are not the sole individual with aspirations and ambitions, yet your objectives appear to be excessively ambitious to be realized. While they may contribute to a favorable outcome in the broader scope, it is crucial to acknowledge that based on your current objectives, you are positioning yourself for potential disappointment and lack of success. Are you pondering the methods by which you can establish goals that are readily attainable? Let us now examine different approaches to establish achievable objectives that will motivate proactive efforts towards a more significant outcome.

Maintain a Clear Objective

When starting out with your goals, having a clear focus on where you want the efforts to end up is important. While you may not initially strive for the highest accolade, having a overarching objective will facilitate your pursuit of the smaller milestones you have established. Although the outcome may not be characterized by extravagant embellishments, maintaining a strong emphasis will still enhance your ability to accomplish more. Maintain a concentrated central purpose on the ultimate outcome, and you will perceive the gratification derived from gradually advancing towards it.

Divide the overarching accomplishment into individual components.

I have subtly alluded to this suggestion earlier; however, by subdividing the ultimate objective into smaller components, you are facilitating a gradual progression towards its achievement, thereby alleviating the overwhelming pressure of tackling the entirety simultaneously. When confronted with an excessive workload, individuals frequently experience feelings of stress, which in turn elicit an immediate inclination towards surrender. By setting incremental objectives, one can effectively manage stress levels and progress steadily towards the ultimate goal.

Establish Realistic Timeframes for Your Objectives

Attempting to perform a task at an excessively leisurely or expeditious pace can significantly disrupt your concentration. Based on the desired outcome, it is crucial to allocate oneself a sufficient amount of time to achieve the objective, ensuring the intended results are attained. As an illustration, it would be prudent to avoid allocating an excessive amount of time for the completion of a minuscule objective, especially when it can be readily achieved within a considerably briefer duration. Exercise rationality and establish logical timelines for both your objectives and accomplishments.

Stack Your Goals

By adopting a sequential approach to your goals, you are simultaneously embarking on a fresh objective while completing the current one you are focused on. This will facilitate the progression to the subsequent stage while concurrently completing the preceding stage. Through this approach, you are ensuring the smooth continuity of the overarching objective, avoiding the stagnation of progress while awaiting the completion of each preceding goal before commencing the next one. Have a clear vision of your future objectives and devote all your endeavors towards achieving them, while ensuring the completion of your current tasks.

Transition to fresh objectives once you sense that you have successfully attained your previously established goal.

On occasion, we may experience a sense of stagnation upon the attainment of a predetermined objective. This situation is disheartening as we are presently at a standstill, and furthermore, we are apprehensive about proceeding to the subsequent stage. Suppose we are not truly prepared to advance? Suppose we still have pending tasks related to our prior objectives. Refuse to allow your uncertainties impede your progress. Commence the pursuit of fresh objectives once you perceive a near-mastery of your prior goals.

Establish Key Performance Indicators to Ensure Personal Responsibility

Regularly assess your own state. Establishing a systematic timetable for monitoring the advancement of your objectives will facilitate comprehension of your current position and identify the subsequent areas requiring attention. Establish a regular schedule designated for self-evaluation, and ensure utmost honesty in assessing your personal growth and accomplishments. By implementing established standards, you will find that you can effectively assess both your achievements and areas for improvement consistently and regularly.

Establishing concrete and attainable objectives will enable you to maximize your endeavors in acquiring new skills or cultivating positive habits. Given the demands of your busy schedule, establishing clear objectives and a coherent vision for your professional aspirations will facilitate your progress in your professional endeavors. Merely being occupied should not be perceived as an impediment to dedicating time towards enhancing your skills. It simply requires concentration and a substantial amount of time.

Devise a Strategic Work Plan and Generate Daily Action Agendas

"Grant me a time frame of six hours to fell a tree, and my initial four hours shall be dedicated to honing the blade of the axe." - Abraham Lincoln

This quotation implicitly underscores the significance of premeditating one's endeavors prior to their execution.

To provide further elucidation, let us briefly delve into the importance of diligently strategizing your tasks.

The Significance of Strategic Work Planning

The renowned 19th-century French poet, novelist, and dramatist, Victor Hugo, eloquently expressed

The individual who diligently strategizes the day's proceedings each morning, meticulously executing that blueprint, possesses a lifeline that shall navigate him through the intricate complexities of even the most demanding existence. But where no plan is laid, where the disposal of time is surrendered merely to the chance of incidence, chaos will soon reign."

A considerable number of individuals struggle to effectively manage their time due to the absence of premeditating their tasks. Rather than formulating a strategy and executing it, we engage in the task without any premeditated plan. Regrettably, this is the reason why we encounter challenges while undertaking a task - due to a lack of strategic planning and the failure to anticipate and address potential obstacles that may arise during its execution.

Through proactive organization and preemptive preparation, one equips oneself for the forthcoming undertaking. You carefully undertake the task, comprehending its scope and requirements, formulating an effective approach and proactively evaluating potential pitfalls and challenges. This assists you in better preparing for any potential outcome.

In order to effectively utilize one's time, it is imperative to acquire proficiency in the skill of strategic planning, as it serves as the foundational practice and inclination that necessitate attention. Allow me to provide you with the necessary instructions for accomplishing that task.

Strategies for Organizing Your Tasks and Establishing Daily Action Plans

By adhering to the provided guidelines, you can ensure that significant tasks are never left unfinished in the future.

Step 1: Determine the tasks that require attention.

Firstly, make a list of all the tasks that need doing within a specified time, say a week. Include all sorts of important and unimportant chores in the list, from grocery shopping to completing an important project report at work, to attending your child's monthly parent teacher meeting at school.

Ensure that these tasks are completed no later than the evening preceding the scheduled day of commencement. Engaging in prior day planning provides a comprehensive outlook on the forthcoming day's sequence of events.

Secondly, I propose identifying tasks of utmost importance.

"The fundamental principle of self-discipline lies in prioritizing tasks of significance over those that are immediate." - Barry Werner

Once the process of compiling the list has been completed, proceed to differentiate the high priority tasks from the low priority tasks. Tasks of utmost importance are the essential responsibilities that require your immediate attention. Given the impending deadline for a work presentation and the need to attend to laundry, which task do you deem to be of greater significance? Certainly, the task of working on the presentation takes precedence (although the circumstances may vary).

Consider the relative significance of various tasks in conjunction with one another and evaluate how each task impacts your overall productivity. Consolidate the crucial tasks aimed at enhancing productivity – these tasks, deemed of high importance, should be undertaken as a priority.

By prioritizing high importance tasks, you can effectively enhance your productivity in an instant. Consequently, your motivation is heightened and you become fully prepared to attain your objectives.

Step 3: Construct a Daily Action Plan

After completing the process of identifying your top-priority tasks and gaining an understanding of the less significant ones, proceed to establish a comprehensive weekly action plan. Having a daily schedule provides a comprehensive overview of the tasks to be accomplished in a day, facilitating efficient work by eliminating the need to allocate time for planning since it is already taken care of.

When formulating a daily itinerary, designate one to two tasks of utmost importance and immediate urgency that necessitate immediate attention, in addition to tasks aimed at enhancing productivity, as well as one or two routine tasks of lower priority, such as tidying one's residence or procuring/organizing groceries.

Allot the designated time during the commencement of your day, or any other period wherein you acknowledge your utmost productivity and alertness, to address the task of highest importance and complexity. Numerous time management authorities, such as Brian Tracy, commonly cite this approach as "tackling the most challenging task first thing in the morning."

Commencing the day with a particularly demanding endeavor reinforces one's commitment to accomplishing significant tasks. Upon the successful completion of this undertaking, one's motivation is likely to surge significantly, as the ability to overcome formidable challenges lends itself to the belief that any subsequent task can be triumphed over.

Reserve less demanding and more pleasurable assignments for the conclusion, much like a delectable reward that follows a day of strenuous labor. Engaging in these activities facilitates relaxation while concurrently enhancing your overall productivity. Take grocery shopping into consideration as an example, where you may conveniently engage in this activity while commuting back from work if you have an affinity for shopping.

Devise daily action plans for a week and endeavor to enhance them each evening.

If you had assigned three important tasks for Tuesday, but you somehow ended up doing one of them on Monday, you should create a new action plan for Tuesday.

One can establish distinct To-do lists for tasks pertaining to work and personal matters in order to avoid any blending of the two domains and effectively manage both personal and professional responsibilities.

Step four involves the definition and specification of your tasks.

When formulating a daily agenda, it is imperative to precisely articulate and delineate the nature of each individual task. Please provide an exposition about the nature of the assigned task, delineate the rationale behind its execution, elucidate the specific requirements inherent in its undertaking, and expound upon your proposed approach to successfully accomplish said task. This effectively transforms a basic task into a refined and well-defined one, resulting in enhanced clarity for you.

As an example, providing a detailed account such as "conducting thorough research on the content and objectives of the upcoming office presentation, precisely defining them, compiling a comprehensive report, and preparing a PowerPoint presentation accordingly" would offer a more explicit depiction of the task at hand, as opposed to a general statement like "working on the next office presentation." The former articulates precisely the specific actions that are required. Include the section detailing the procedural steps for each task beneath it, ensuring precise comprehension of the execution process.

In order to successfully accomplish your list of tasks and implement your action plans, it is essential to assign a specific deadline to each individual task. Allow us to discuss the significance of this established practice and elaborate on the methodology in the upcoming chapter.

Beat It!

There exists no further opportunity to retreat. It is imperative that you take immediate action while considering the adage "Seize the moment." This matter does not possess a predetermined expiration, yet it is consistently advantageous to execute it promptly once prepared. You have already amassed your reflections, implemented a transformation in your perspectives towards obstacles and limitations. Why would one initiate their development if there is no intention to employ them for their intended purpose? Time is ticking!

Rise and Alter Your Perspective

You possess an already well-established and immaculate foundation to commence from; hence, allow me to present a scenario for contemplation.

Envision a scenario in which you possess significant wealth. In the near future, you intend to procure a high-end automobile, as your financial resources are sufficient to facilitate such a purchase. You stored the funds within a password-protected vault. You possess exclusive knowledge of the password and have chosen not to disclose it to any other individual. Your funds are ample to acquire and sustain a high-end automobile.

On a particular day, you elect to remain in bed, basking in the comforts of your opulent existence, when your sister enters your chambers. Your sister has requested that you promptly make the purchase of the vehicle. You responded in the affirmative, yet remained stationary. After a considerable passage of time, whilst indulging in your leisurely repose upon the bed, your child enters the room and beseeches you for the same, expressing the necessity of its usage. You provided an affirmative response in response. Evening has arrived and you remain in your bedding. You were in such a state of elation that you remained oblivious to the fact that the day was nearing its conclusion. Suddenly, your mother came into your room and asked you to buy the car because she needs it as well. You affirmed her request, yet you did not rise and relocate until the conclusion of the day.

Do you anticipate successfully completing the purchase of the car? I would say no. Regardless of the number of individuals who attempt to assist you through requests, commands, instructions, or even pleas, it remains inconsequential. If you persist in engaged in verbal discourse without taking action, you will not accomplish anything.

Your family and dear ones are indeed present. They likely exerted their utmost efforts to aid in your extraction from seclusion, however, should you persist in refraining from emerging and engaging, you will ultimately accomplish naught.

This should be considered the initial and paramount task that must be undertaken. You must relinquish your previous thought patterns and develop an entirely new paradigm. This process may be time-consuming and demands diligent effort; however, it is imperative to recognize that if one is unable to alter their behavior, they cannot expect to initiate a transformation in their persona. You have to consider that the whole world will change around you if you change your mindset.

In altering your mindset, it is imperative to navigate through a myriad of potential pitfalls, issues, and impediments. The primary and likely the most arduous barrier you will encounter pertains to your personal incapacity to adopt a different lifestyle. We, as individuals, exhibit a general aversion towards change, regardless of its magnitude. Transitions consistently bring about a significant level of comprehension and incredulity. We make considerable efforts to eschew change and consistently engage in opposition to it. In the majority of instances, the specific circumstances hold little significance - whether it pertains to altering the brand of your toothbrush or transforming your entire way of living. If you possess a fondness for a particular way of life, an extensive amount of exertion is indispensable to effectuate any changes.

Many of us fail to comprehend that we are not leading lives that are optimal in nature. Certainly, certain elements are observable, such as the physical dimensions of our existence, but the cognitive dimensions of our lives often go largely unnoticed.

It is evident that we have experienced weight gain and necessitate physical activity to reduce the excess weight. Nonetheless, comprehending the need for a corresponding shift in our mental disposition towards life poses a challenge. It diverges from the realm of the tangible, yet assumes heightened significance.

In order for you to undergo a transformation, it is imperative that you acquire and develop a sense of self-discipline. I possess sufficient knowledge on the topic of self-discipline to compose an entire book elucidating its transformative impact on individuals. However, I shall merely provide a succinct overview of the subject matter at hand in due course. Currently, it is imperative that you comprehend the necessity of possessing self-discipline, and the sooner you commence your efforts towards acquiring it, the more advantageous it shall be for you.

Principle 1:

Understanding Time Optimization

The reality is that the leisure time one carves out in life bears a direct relationship to the amount of time invested in engaging in activities that genuinely bring joy. Hence, the primary principle in chronological order is Optimization.

The maximization of time is fundamental yet highly efficacious in the diligent management of a fulfilling existence. Absence of a profound comprehension of temporal management renders the possession of 30 hours of leisure per week entirely futile. This book serves as a comprehensive guide to improving your calendar, leading to an enhanced quality of life.

The initial chapter of Taking Control of Time is focused on comprehending the concept of time and employing the first technique to construct a life that is embraced, rather than a life that is merely expended. The primary takeaway from chapter one lies in the importance of assuming command over time, enabling the opportunity to allocate it according to one's preferences.

Time optimization can be divided into two fundamental principles that, when put into practice, allow for the efficient allocation of time, consequently enhancing the economic value per hour and reducing the length of the workday.

"The first principle of temporal optimization:

Efficient execution of elementary tasks can be achieved by employing software automation or by undertaking deliberate and repetitive actions. Illustrations of such types of tasks encompass monotonous and laborious manual work. These tasks comprise of documentation, data entry, dishwashing, house cleaning, and so forth.

The proposed resolution entails consistently directing one's attention towards expediting the completion of uncomplicated tasks. Conducting extensive research using specialized software and delegating these tasks to cost-effective virtual assistants. If an assignment necessitates individual effort, consider transforming it into a stimulating endeavor by striving to accomplish each objective with utmost efficiency. This approach not only injects a sense of enthusiasm into mundane tasks but also facilitates swift completion when contrasted with a more relaxed work routine.

"The Second Law of Temporal Optimization:

Using creative thinking to implement time saving solutions for dynamic tasks. In the realm of productivity, innovative thinking serves as the ultimate disruptor of a hectic agenda. The responsibilities that entail the need for inventive thought encompass writing, amalgamation, decision-making, and formulating viable solutions.

The Solutions:

Proposal 1: The objective is to employ innovative methods to systematically disassemble complex, ever-changing tasks into manageable components that can be effortlessly executed. Once these tasks are broken down, they can be incorporated into your list of straightforward tasks. It is imperative to decompose the tasks into elementary actions in order to apply the principle of time optimization.

Alternative 2: Employ reverse engineering as a means to efficiently resolve issues. By honing your mental acuity to swiftly and efficiently generate solutions for ever-changing tasks, you will significantly optimize your workflow. The crucial aspect of this workflow lies in the ability to mentally envision your experience as you carried out the task, and subsequently backtrack the actions you executed in order to efficiently and expediently accomplish the complex task at hand. This approach may necessitate a slightly longer period of time for mastery; however, diligently honing your cognitive abilities to swiftly tackle challenges will prove to be your greatest advantage in combating time constraints.

Consequently, the initial chapter delves into the first two tenets of temporal dynamics.

The first aspect pertains to expediting task completion with the aim of maximizing monetary gains in the shortest possible time frame. The second aspect pertains to the utilization of the available leisure time.

Dealing With Distractions

Maintaining focused concentration is of utmost importance when actively striving to conserve precious moments for the purpose of achieving something significant. How about we take a gander at how you can manage interruptions better. Assuming control of your time and concentration.

Accquiring the expertise of effectively managing time in board meetings is achievable through training. It encompasses the compilation of your assignments and monitoring your progress. We should commence the discussion by addressing the organization aspect. Organizing your tasks

There are multiple methodologies at your disposal to organize your tasks efficiently. Two of the noteworthy ones include the Eisenhower decision matrix and the ABCDE technique. The Eisenhower choice matrix

The choice grid technique derives its name from the ex-U.S. president and is predicated on a statement attributed to him: "I encounter two distinct categories of concerns: those that are of grave importance and those that are truly significant." The trivial matters hold little importance, while the important matters are seldom urgent." To organize your tasks using this approach, you categorize them into four quadrants: important and urgent; important, but not urgent; urgent, but not important; neither important nor urgent. We should examine each of these quadrants.

Immediate and consequential: As implied by their name, these tasks must be swiftly and diligently addressed, as their prompt completion carries paramount importance as well. In this section, you will primarily allocate all the tasks that carry the highest level of importance.

Significant, yet not obligatory: This quadrant shall encompass all the tasks that ought to be accomplished within the specified time frame (be it a day or a week, or any other designated period). These tasks are of utmost importance, albeit not necessarily occupying the topmost position on your priority list.

Immediate, non-substantial: This particular class usually consists of assignments that relate to ourselves or individuals within our network. However, if completed now, it may detract valuable time from more significant tasks. Assignments that can be further delegated pertain to this category.

In both personal and professional domains, certain tasks should not occupy our agenda, though they manage to find their way onto it, insignificant and noncritical as they may be. This specific quadrant consists of a multitude of tasks that should unequivocally be eradicated from your list of assignments.

The ABCDE method

This approach bears striking resemblance to the Eisenhower grid across multiple dimensions. Moreover, due to its significance, the grade is assigned to the err. In this framework, you assign a score to a task that is challenging or directly impacts your goals and objectives. A Level B assignment denotes tasks of a moderate degree of importance, but their completion does not significantly impact one's personal or professional livelihoods if left undone. Any task categorized with a Grade C rating is considered discretionary, as it does not entail any penalties should you choose not to complete them. Correspondence that can be dispatched to others belongs to the Grade D category. Furthermore, errands that can be readily removed from your schedule without any significant complications should be placed in the Grade E classification.

Conducting an evaluation of the time needed for each task

Another aspect of organizing oneself involves cultivating an understanding of the duration required for each task within one's schedule.

The hierarchical method

One method of evaluating is to determine the overall time required for a task. This approach, commonly referred to as the hierarchical technique, proves to be advantageous in cases where it is challenging or intricate to accurately estimate the time required for each task within a project. Instead of becoming overly preoccupied with such nuances, you may consider relying on a comprehensive estimate of the usual duration it takes for either yourself or others to finish the task.

The base up method

Something that goes against the established hierarchical approach, commonly referred to as a bottom-up strategy. In this methodology, you divide the task into smaller segments and estimate the optimal time for each. In order to create gauges, one must disseminate the intricacies of all the tasks. Undoubtedly, the accuracy will be enhanced with this approach.

Avoiding distractions

A timetable can provide assistance, provided that one is committed to adhering to it. One of the main challenges encountered while maintaining your schedule is effectively managing disruptions. In contemporary times, one of the most effortless means of becoming engaged is by receiving a notification on your mobile device. Paradoxically, the devices that are meant to enhance our lives can also complicate them. Upon taking an objective perspective, it is evident that your telephone serves as a reliable means of communication, and therefore, it is advisable to keep it in your possession to ensure a continued connection with the world. The pervasive nature of mobile phones necessitates our diligent handling to address its implications. This preferential treatment denotes that whenever we engage in a different task and receive a phone call, we are obligated to address it, even if it necessitates interrupting the truly significant matter at hand. To address the matter pertaining to the phone, initiate the process by disabling any notifications during periods of significant tasks or responsibilities. This will put an end to the influence others have on your decision-making process. Instead of allowing yourself to become distracted by your online media or email application, it is advisable to wait until the task at hand has been completed. Should you find it uncomfortable to deactivate all warnings, you may selectively disable those that are specifically related to recreational activities.

Occasionally, an objective assessment of the duration you allocate to your telephone usage can yield the desired realization. An application such as ScreenTime provides an estimation of the amount of time you spend on your mobile device, including the applications that you use most frequently. This can help

you do a self-assessment of how much time you stay diverted. The application also boasts an additional advantageous feature - it allows you to restrict your usage time on a given application.

In addition to your mobile phone and various electronic devices, the environmental conditions in which you reside or operate may also induce distraction. The precise remedies for the disruption will naturally vary depending on the specific circumstances. As an illustration, if the matter at hand pertains to noisy coworkers, one may consider employing noise-canceling headphones as a potential solution. Music also serves as a resource that caters to individuals within specific contexts.

Eliminating procrastination

Procrastination is a matter that affects each and every one of us. Arguably, the most detrimental aspect of procrastination is its enduring nature. In general, lingerings manifest themselves in various formats.

Occasionally, we remain in contemplation due to the realization that the task at hand does not possess an urgent nature. Rather than focusing on that assignment, leave the attention on those undertakings that are dire. One way to overcome this type of hesitation is by reminding yourself of the importance of the task you are neglecting. For example, if the task at hand is to efficiently organize your schedule and eliminate unnecessary obligations, contemplate how the time saved will grant you the opportunity to pursue a long-awaited endeavor that has eluded your schedule thus far. It could potentially be attributed to the juxtaposition between acquiring newfound skills, dedicating time to your loved ones, or allocating more time to your secondary professional pursuit.

An additional rationale for our prolonged stay is rooted in our apprehension of experiencing letdown. This often leads individuals who have set high expectations for themselves to subsequently experience a state of distress upon realizing their inability to maintain said standards. One possible strategy for addressing this matter is to perceive oneself as more than an individual responsible solely for achieving at the utmost level. This will allow you to disassociate your self-worth from your level of achievement.

The third explanation is also a customary one, stemming from our reluctance to engage in productive labor. According to our hierarchy of priorities, happiness takes precedence over work. Our primary objective is not to avoid completing the task, but rather to prioritize seeking and experiencing joy at this present moment, with the intention of completing the work at a later time. It is imperative for individuals categorized in this group to place significance on the same approach of considering the broader context. Are you able to attend to the tasks following engagement in enjoyable activities, or would it be more prudent to first complete the work and subsequently indulge in leisure?

The overarching approach to addressing procrastination is to commence each day by tackling the most challenging task you will encounter on a daily basis. This methodology is called the Eat the Frog approach, which takes its name from a renowned Mark Twain quote that suggests if one needs to consume a live amphibian, it would be more strategic to do so as a priority. Evidently, commencing with this task might not be the most opportune moment for all individuals. Therefore, an additional refinement we can incorporate into this strategy is to allocate our resources to a period that holds greater potential for general utility throughout the day.

It is imperative to acknowledge in this context that not all procrastination is detrimental. Occasionally engaging in deliberate delays can be advantageous as it provides an opportunity to explore matters from a fresh standpoint and consequently enhance the progress of one's work. The pivotal aspect lies in ensuring that one refrains from excessive hesitancy, as it may result in an insufficient amount of time remaining to complete one's assigned tasks.

Identifying your peak hours

As aforementioned, there are specific instances wherein your

usefulness tops. Irrespective of whether you are overseeing professional responsibilities or personal affairs, acknowledging these peak periods of productivity can yield significant results. By capitalizing on these opportune moments, you can enhance your task completion and, consequently, avoid prolonging tasks and experiencing frustration.

Exploring the periods during which you are most productive is a captivating endeavor. For instance, there are instances wherein the time when an individual is most productive does not necessarily align with their employer's designated working hours. In addition to each individual experiencing their prolonged periods of peak productivity, there are also several attributes that we all have in common when it comes to being productive. According to the renowned researcher Nathaniel Kleitman, who discovered the 90-minute rest-activity cycle that occurs during our sleep, individuals also experience a 90-minute rhythm during which they transition from states of heightened awareness to periods of decreased alertness.

When reflecting upon your prime periods of productivity, you may be tempted to reminisce, but it is advisable to adopt a more systematic approach. One method to accomplish this entails creating a comprehensive record of one's activities for the entire week, followed by self-assessment on a daily basis using a predefined scale. You may also consider soliciting guidance from individuals who have already successfully implemented this approach. Presented here is an article authored by Chris Bailey and published in A Life of Productivity, wherein he analyzes the process of determining one's biological prime time.

Therefore, what factors should you consider when enhancing your productivity?

Based on the calculations conducted by Chris, it is advisable to assess the levels of your energy, concentration, and inspiration throughout the day. When given an extensive amount of information, one will be able to discern if certain patterns are emerging.

How can one effectively handle or oversee the results derived from computational processes? How can you harness your utmost efficiency?

The most optimal utilization of your most valuable time would entail dedicating it towards challenging tasks that require analytical thinking and decision-making pertaining to significant matters. The heightened levels of vitality, motivation, and concentration facilitate the management of tasks with greater ease. Clearly, from a functional standpoint, it can be arduous to abstain from undertaking less demanding tasks during your busiest periods, particularly if they are urgent and assigned to you by a superior at your place of employment. However, the objective is to avoid striving for perfection and focus on effectively handling as many significant tasks as feasible during the peak hours.

Thus far, we have delved into the various ways in which you can be generally beneficial. Equally important is to pay attention to the instances in which your utility may be limited. In an ideal scenario, it is advisable to allocate this time towards tasks that do not require an equivalent level of concentration.

Time Management Skills

Have you ever pondered upon the efficaciousness with which certain individuals accomplish all their tasks while you find yourself frantically scurrying to and fro, overwhelmed by anxiety? In the present era, effective time management abilities hold significant importance. By integrating these skills into your everyday activities, you will discover that accomplishing all tasks is well within your reach.

Unlocking the Secrets of Effective Time Management

As previously mentioned, duties can be classified into three primary divisions: Urgent, Significant, and Insignificant. High-priority tasks necessitate prompt resolution, while significant tasks require diligent attention.

For example:

Urgent: Answer the phone. It could potentially be your supervisor contacting you to inquire about the progress of the report he had requested previously, or alternatively, it is plausible that an individual engaged in cold-calling may be contacting you with regards to double-glaze windows. You will only ascertain its nature once you attend to the phone call.

It is imperative to seek medical attention should one be experiencing any signs of illness. Ensuring the preservation of your well-being is of utmost significance, and failure to seek medical attention when you are unwell could potentially culminate in the development of a significantly more grave condition. Seek medical attention promptly to prevent the condition from worsening.

Critical and significant: The task of picking up the children from school belongs to the critical and significant categories, as failing to do so would leave them unattended, causing distress and potentially leading to legal intervention with severe ramifications.

Not Important: Reading what your friends are doing on Facebook is most certainly not important, especially when you're supposed to be working. Please attend to your personal emails either during your allocated lunch break or subsequent to completing your work assignment.

It is evident that by allocating your tasks into these categories, you will effectively manage your time to accomplish them. This is applicable in both professional and personal domains.

It is imperative that you prioritize the well-being of your health as you manage your schedule. After a duration of 45 minutes of remaining seated at your workstation, it is advisable to rise and engage in ambulatory activities for a period of ten minutes.

Please be advised that your Urgent, Important, and Not Important tasks may undergo frequent fluctuations on an hourly, daily, and weekly basis. The priorities that hold significance at 8:30 am may undergo alteration by 1 pm. Hence, it is advisable that you revise your To Do list whenever a task transitions from being Important to Urgent, or from Not Important to

Important. In addition, it is imperative to deliberate upon the true sense of urgency or significance, as well as ascertain whether such tasks necessitate your personal attention. If that is not the case, then perhaps you should contemplate the idea of bestowing it upon another individual.

Supplementary Tenets for Effective Time Management

Keep tidy

Operating in an untidy environment not only elicits feelings of workplace despair, but also hinders organizational proficiency and focus, thereby impeding task accomplishment. Maintaining a clean and organized workplace not only fosters a sense of self-worth and enhances one's self-drive, but also facilitates adherence to one's schedule.

Pick Your Moment

Consistently strategize the scheduling of your tasks within appropriate timeframes. As an illustration, it is advisable to refrain from arranging a meeting for 9am if one is aware of the fact that they typically arrive at the office at 8.45am and require the consumption of three cups of coffee to stimulate their cognitive abilities early in the morning. Coordinate crucial meetings or perform timely errands such as delivering mail.

An additional valuable suggestion includes prioritizing minor yet significant responsibilities, such as corresponding with the HR department or the school administration, during brief intervals preceding meetings and appointments.

Don't Procrastinate

At times, the tendency to delay obligations affects everyone; despite the necessity to complete a task, it is inexplicable why we still choose to defer it. Procrastination is a detrimental force that steals away our precious time, as the proverbial adage suggests. If you possess significant or pressing responsibilities that require completion, and you continue to attempt to postpone them, it is imperative that you ascertain the underlying cause for such behavior. Do you possess the necessary confidence in your abilities to successfully accomplish the task? Do you have any doubts regarding the ethical implications of the task at hand? Do you believe that an alternative approach should be considered? If any of these assertions are accurate, I encourage you to seek guidance from a fellow professional, a higher-ranking individual, or a trusted family member to explore alternative possibilities.

Don't Attempt to Multi-task

While it is true that certain individuals claim to possess the ability to effortlessly engage in multiple tasks simultaneously, the reality is that multi-tasking, more often than not, does not possess the favorable attributes often attributed to it. As previously stated, the human brain is inherently wired to concern itself with unresolved matters. Hence, it is significantly more advisable to complete a task, ensuring thoroughness, before transitioning to another assignment.

Stay Calm

The most effective advice with regards to time management is to consistently maintain a calm demeanor. When faced with a multitude of tasks and a limited timeframe for completion, it is common to experience feelings of stress and being inundated. Regardless of whether or not you accomplish these tasks, the world will not come to an end. Prioritizing one's health and ensuring adequate rest should take precedence over staying awake all night, experiencing stress due to a relatively less significant deadline for a task.

Displaying The Appropriate Attitude And Mindset

Effective time management is imperative for maximizing productivity. Having the ability to proficiently and productively organize your time serves as a solid basis for attaining your objectives and generating results. By effectively managing one's time, greater productivity can be achieved within a limited timeframe.

It is highly manageable to adhere to regulations and have a clear understanding of the dos and don'ts pertaining to effectively managing one's time. In the interim, it is imperative to acquire a fundamental understanding of the prerequisites essential for accomplishing this objective, namely possessing the appropriate disposition and perspective. In any undertaking, the approach you employ will greatly shape the outcomes and the influence you leave behind. Consequently, in order to effectively oversee one's time, it becomes imperative to eradicate any detrimental or restrictive convictions that may hinder or sway an individual, and instead, adopt affirmative and empowering ideologies.

To commence the endeavor of managing your time effectively, presented below are methods through which you can imbue, foster, and uphold a favorable and enabling mental stance and disposition concerning time, productivity, and work on the whole.

1. Be realistic.

Frequently, individuals become engrossed in a multitude of tasks and objectives. If you happen to fall into this category, it is likely that you are well aware of the fact that populating your agenda with an excessive number of tasks can present a formidable challenge. In order to enhance productivity and optimize efficiency, it is advisable to maintain a high level of realism.

In order to adhere to a realistic approach towards managing your time, it would be advisable to consider the duration it typically takes to accomplish a given task and preserve honesty in this assessment. Frequently, individuals have a tendency to conceive of concepts based on ideals rather than considering the practicality of their current circumstances. For example, when composing a task list, there is often a temptation to hastily jot down numerous activities intended to be completed within a single day, attempting to maximize efficiency. Nevertheless, individuals are not automatons, and one's capabilities are inherently limited.

Practicing pragmatism involves addressing objectives that you possess certainty of successfully achieving within a specified timeframe. This will afford you greater opportunities for concentration and the execution of your utmost efforts.

2. Be open and flexible.

Undoubtedly, possessing a flexible and open mindset is a crucial component in the formula for achieving success.

The attributes of receptiveness and adaptability enable individuals to effectively respond to novel circumstances and engage in heightened personal growth. In the realm of time management, adopting such dispositions will effectively augment your level of productivity, while concurrently fostering improved prospects for both your personal and professional endeavors.

Frequently, individuals adhere to plans and objectives without any inclination to adapt and modify them if required. Similarly, concerning approaches and procedures, individuals are excessively accustomed to a particular framework or methodology, thereby perceiving the introduction of change as a barrier to efficiency.

For example, individuals accustomed to performing tasks manually may feel apprehensive about utilizing computer technology. They opt to retain archaic methodologies and exhibit resistance towards acquiring contemporary proficiencies - specifically, acquainting themselves with fundamental computer literacy. They employ age as a rationale, yet fundamentally, can one truly claim that anyone is too advanced in years to acquire computer literacy?

Possessing such a demeanor effectively hinders individuals from acquiring knowledge and embracing innovative approaches that could significantly enhance productivity. Maintaining a receptive mindset enables one to effectively manage their time, particularly when their current approach is no longer yielding desirable results.

Additionally, possessing an attitude of openness and adaptability holds utmost significance in regards to scheduling and strategic planning. It is an indisputable fact that certain predetermined activities and events often fail to materialize as intended. Regardless of how conscientious one may be in managing their time, the unfolding of events remains outside their sphere of influence. Rather than berating yourself, it is important to acknowledge that various external factors contribute to the outcome of things. Being adaptable and receptive entails recognizing these variables and exerting additional effort to offer some flexibility or contingency in the event that certain plans do not materialize, maintaining alternative options such as a backup plan or even a secondary contingency plan.

3. Do not overcommit

Time is a valuable resource, and the allocation of this resource can heavily influence one's productivity outcomes. Rather than placing emphasis on quantity, it would be more advantageous to direct our attention towards the aspect of quality. As the adage suggests, "Employ efficient strategies rather than exhaustive efforts." This implies the importance of avoiding excessive commitments and overwhelming tasks. Taking on more than one can handle can have adverse effects on the attainment of desired outcomes and objectives.

Exercise discretion by exclusively undertaking tasks within your realm of knowledge and ensuring timely completion. This entails possessing the sagacity and audacity to decline. The ability to decline empowers you to give precedence to certain aspects within your agenda that hold greater significance to you. One may opt to prioritize quality time with their family instead of working additional hours, or make the decision to forgo attending a high school reunion in order to participate in a significant meeting or seminar. Subjecting oneself to excessive commitments displays an insufficiency in the ability to prioritize effectively. Possess a clear understanding of your priorities and discern the activities and endeavors that merit your valuable time and effort to enhance your overall productivity.

4. Perfection is a myth

Attaining perfection is an elusive concept, a construct of our imaginative faculties. The concept of perfection is inherently subjective, thus making it open to wide interpretation. Proficient practitioners of time management steer clear of the pitfall known as "perfection paralysis." This phenomenon entails an overwhelming desire to achieve flawlessness in every task, resulting in a pause or postponement of work, ultimately leading to minimal or no progress.

Indeed, it is an undeniable fact that emphasis should be placed on the significance of quality over quantity, especially when it comes to undertaking specific responsibilities and determining priorities. In the interim, with regards to carrying out the tasks at hand, it is advisable to adopt a proactive approach and engage in actions that can yield concrete outcomes, as opposed to awaiting an opportune moment or optimal level of motivation.

Becoming entangled in the pursuit of perfection could lead to your stagnation. It is advisable to commence your task even if you anticipate that the outcome may not manifest as the epitome of perfection.

For example, in the case of individuals who engage in the craft of writing, a common challenge encountered is commonly referred to as "writer's block." This phenomenon extends beyond mere absence of creative stimulation, encompassing also a manifestation of uncertainty and occasionally demoralization. In lieu of heeding the admonitions of your internal detractor and striving to evade any errors, exert your utmost efforts to engage in writing, initially disregarding technical considerations such as grammar and structure. Those tasks are designated for the process of editing, which occurs subsequent to the act of writing. Rather than awaiting the elusive arrival of writing inspiration or motivation, simply commence writing without concern for the perceived perfection of your prose. Upon acquiring something, the process of editing and revising becomes significantly more convenient. This methodology can be implemented in conjunction with various other forms of work.

Please be reminded that perfection does not exist. It is highly improbable to achieve perfection on the initial attempt. It is more convenient to modify, polish, amend, or restructure an existing entity rather than anticipating the emergence of perfection on an empty canvas.

Recognizing and acknowledging that absolute perfection is unattainable will enable you to enhance your performance, effectively allocate your time, and achieve optimal productivity.

5. Get into action

This perspective aligns with the aforementioned viewpoint: the notion of perfection is an illusion. Taking proactive measures yields further actions, whereas passivity begets more passivity. It is one matter to devise and arrange, it is an entirely separate matter to commence execution and undertake the tasks at hand.

Efficiently strategizing is merely one facet of effective time management. The productivity and success are genuinely dependent on the execution of these plans and tasks. To effectively administer one's time, it is imperative to cease procrastination and commence engaging in tasks promptly.

Maintain a consistent frame of mind characterized by proactive thinking and a resolute and unwavering approach, and you will confidently progress towards achieving productivity and attaining success.

6. Have a growth mindset

The effective utilization of one's time encompasses the progression and enhancement of one's abilities. Ultimately, the results you attain hold significance, irrespective of their seeming triviality, such as the act of dispatching electronic correspondence. Inevitably, one task begets another.

Adopting a growth-oriented mindset will facilitate your progression from point A to B, while enabling you to achieve all desired goals. Being a proficient time manager necessitates the ability to discern one's priorities, recognize significant matters, evaluate their effectiveness, and allocate the requisite time and attention accordingly.

7. Focus on value

The crux of effective time management lies in striking a harmonious equilibrium between efficiency and effectiveness.

Efficiency refers to the capacity to effectively complete tasks and achieve desired outcomes in the most expeditious and convenient manner possible. In the meantime, effectiveness entails executing tasks in a manner that optimizes outcomes. The optimal point of balance between these two exceptional treasures lies in their value. When one successfully achieves both efficiency and effectiveness, it is evident that value is being added and commendable work is being executed, irrespective of the nature of the endeavor.

Intentional Time Management Solution

In order to achieve success in life, it is imperative to adopt a deliberate and systematic approach to time management. Intentional refers to a deliberate and purposeful force that is set in motion through thoughtful planning. This implies the necessity of cultivating constructive behaviors, conduct, cognition, and routines in order to maximize the worth of our time. Life is replete with fluctuations and if one fails to effectively manage their time, they are bound to experience deterioration. It is implausible to effect immediate change on the news we encounter, but we do possess the capacity to alter the news framework in the days yet to come. Engaging in enjoyable activities can be considered a highly effective approach to honing intentional time management skills. If we allocate time for personal self-care, it provides a valuable source of solace and facilitates a state of productivity during our professional pursuits.

In the event of a pessimistic outlook, one may consider adopting rational-emotive imagery as a means to transform perspectives and cultivate rational cognitive capacities, thereby fostering prospects for achievement. The procedure entails visualizing vivid representations of elaborate circumstances, and subsequently engaging in clear-minded introspection regarding the challenges one encounters. In the event that one possesses an optimistic disposition, it would be advantageous to engage in the aforementioned practice, as unforeseen circumstances in life have the potential to foster discouragement. Should you possess apprehension towards facing challenges, engaging in behavioral rehearsals may prove efficacious. Such rehearsals involve the deliberate practice of tasks that elicit fear or anxiety as a direct result of inadequate skills or knowledge. In a professional setting, consider exploring novel endeavors within your workplace that present you with challenges, and diligently strive to accomplish the assigned objectives. This will aid in surmounting challenges, and in the event that your time management strategy proves unsuccessful, you will be equipped to address it in a constructive manner. Resisting obstacles is a prominent impediment that adversely impacts the achievement of success in the lives of numerous individuals. If an acutely rooted fear exists within your psyche, it is probable that it shall manifest itself at a later juncture in your existence. Fear is the underlying cause of failure, as many individuals fail to discern between healthy and unhealthy fears due to a lack of exploration and analysis.

If we are hesitant to embark on new opportunities in life, it is frequently due to our apprehension towards embracing change. Change is good. Transformation demonstrates that progress is in constant flux. Certain changes may have negative implications, although, in general, it is inevitable and necessary to embrace change. As professionals in the realm of business, we frequently bear a significant level of responsibility and frequently encounter diverse sets of requirements. Our responsibilities frequently entail the need to conduct thorough analysis, evaluation, and critical thinking in order to facilitate the implementation of a plan. Frequently, collaboration with individuals is a common practice, consequently resulting in the inevitability of change. Maintaining a high level of concentration can effectively contribute to enhancing business profits, accomplishing our objectives, and effectively managing our time. Our proficiency necessitates our dedication to diligent effort. Effective time management is an integral aspect of daily functioning, and indulging in pessimistic thoughts does not offer a viable strategy for deliberate time allocation.

Typically, individuals form their ideas and thoughts on the basis of assumptions, laboring under the belief that something is imminent, when in reality, it rarely materializes. In times of adversity, the initial step I take is to rise in the morning and affirm to myself that today will be characterized by positivity. I strive to incorporate this mindset into my daily life to the greatest extent feasible. Remarkably, more often than not, favorable outcomes tend to materialize when I affirm this belief to myself. I am cognizant of the fact that the favorable outcomes I have experienced were not solely a consequence of my optimistic words and mindset, but rather a reflection of the diligent efforts and exceptional motivation that have actively contributed to the betterment of my life. I executed an operation within this equation that yielded the results that were presented to me. Hence, if you desire to establish a deliberate time management strategy, you must initiate action to execute your plans. It is imperative that you acquire a constructive approach to managing your daily responsibilities. Do not perceive work as a mere task, but rather perceive it as a means to bring you closer to your objective. If you are dissatisfied with your current employment, endeavor to identify a resolution. You must either accept the situation or seek an alternative that is more preferable. There exists a viable resolution to every predicament.

Gratification
The web entrepreneur experiences a sense of fulfillment and accomplishment upon successfully finishing a task. The feeling of fulfillment serves as an incentive, imparting the necessary inspiration for them to either engage with new customers or rejuvenate their business relationships with existing ones.
These factors frequently serve as motivators for home-based entrepreneurs to effectively manage their time and innovate to increase their productivity. The diligent attention to minutiae in managing a business, such as effectively handling one's time, enables the entrepreneur to tactfully oversee the intricacies of their business affairs.

Nevertheless, there are instances where entrepreneurs may not always experience favorable or uncomplicated circumstances in their endeavors to accomplish various tasks throughout their business ventures. When they bear responsibility for every aspect of their business, there is always the risk of failure or dissatisfaction due to inadequate design or organization. What are the potential consequences that arise when time management proves ineffective or fails to yield the desired outcomes?

Do all internet entrepreneurs face difficulties when it comes to managing their time?

Occasionally, home-based entrepreneurs may find themselves realizing that their systems and procedures are not functioning effectively. They become aware that irrespective of their activities or engagements, they are unable to sustain concentration and successfully accomplish their assigned tasks or objectives. They realize that they are fundamentally mishandling their time and unable to achieve either minor or major objectives. What alternative factors might also be responsible? Ineffectual time management. Inadequate time allocation. Substandard time control. Mismanagement of one's time.

Factors Contributing To Ineffective Time Management

Subpar time management - - Does an internet entrepreneur ever acknowledge that they possess inadequate time management skills? Alternatively, could it be presumed that as a business proprietor, he instinctively assumes he is proficiently and adeptly overseeing his time?

Regardless, he must exercise caution in order to avoid any frivolous behavior or failure to fully leverage the flexible time available to entrepreneurs in employment reception scenarios. In the absence of a proactive endeavor, he could likewise be destined for inadequacy or mere operational downfall.

Often, procrastination is the foremost cause of ineffective time management, yet it is commonly regarded less seriously than the perceived notion of cleverness in delaying tasks. Put differently, internet entrepreneurs often experience apprehension regarding the pace at which they should progress with their business endeavors or how swiftly they should make critical decisions.

Although this may seem honorable, it frequently yields contrary outcomes by inducing work-from-home individuals to exhibit sluggishness, excessive haste, or complete inaction. blast management may help.

Methods To Prevent Overexertion

Occasionally, we exceed our capacities without fully perceiving it. You assent to commitments, assuming that you possess an ample surplus of time. Furthermore, as you strive to fulfill the expectations of those who rely on you, However, it is permissible to decline. It is not possible to be present at multiple places simultaneously, therefore, do not exert yourself attempting to do so. Continuously experiencing stress and excessive work can be detrimental to both your physical and mental well-being. Frequently, individuals request assistance from you as they are reluctant or unwilling to undertake the tasks themselves, understanding that you are likely to acquiesce. However, many of the factors that cause stress or overburden you are within your control and can be rectified.

A good example is:

In the event that a close companion is embarking on a vacation and requires your assistance in tending to their residence by feeding their feline companion and watering their botanical specimens. You desire to extend your assistance, driven by a sense of responsibility owing to their prior support or the strength of your friendship. However, adhering to the timetable would necessitate your presence both in the mornings and evenings. It is evident that carrying out this task on a daily basis will lead to you being unable to reach your workplace punctually and hinder your ability to have breakfast. Additionally, it would be necessary for you to pass by during the evening, thereby impeding your ability to attend the gym. The apparent solution would be to refuse their request, yet you appear to be unable to accomplish that. We all have encountered a similar circumstance previously. Declining their request might create the perception of disappointment on their end, however, prioritizing your own needs is of paramount importance. If the circumstances are such that they would hinder your ability to fulfill your customary activities, then it is inadvisable to proceed.

If you struggle with asserting yourself and find it challenging to decline requests, here are some effective strategies that may assist you:

Kindly inform them that you require ample time to contemplate the matter and carefully review your schedule. Please inform them that you will provide a response at your earliest convenience, should you be able to do so.

Inform them sincerely that you are currently overwhelmed with numerous obligations. If one upholds honesty, it is widely comprehended by the majority.

Recommend that they seek out an alternative individual who may be more suited to providing assistance in accordance with their requirements.

Ultimately, prioritizing self-care should be your foremost concern. If one is experiencing the burden of excessive commitments and operating at maximum capacity, they will have difficulty accomplishing their own assignments. This situation causes you significant distress and will ultimately have a detrimental impact on your well-being. Prioritizing your own needs is not an act of selfishness. If an individual maintains a state of well-being and exhibits a lack of stress, their ability to accomplish tasks will significantly increase.

Through careful foresight and diligent planning, you will develop a more comprehensive grasp on the tasks that must be accomplished. When someone makes a request, it is advisable to carefully assess your existing commitments before committing to their demands. Your priorities should be given precedence and it is important for others to be cognizant of this fact. Once they become cognizant that you shall only accommodate their requests within the confines of your availability, they will demonstrate an increased awareness and consideration of your own requirements as well. On certain occasions, individuals may fail to consider the matters you are attending to, unless you explicitly draw their attention to them. Do not harbor any negative emotions regarding the act of declining their request and articulate the reasons behind your decision.

Prevent the excessive scheduling of your days through the use of a calendar. The format may either be hard copy or electronic (accessible on your personal device or computer); however, please ensure that it is utilized.

Please be mindful that certain tasks may require more time to complete and it is advisable to consistently request an estimate regarding their duration. This can facilitate the determination of whether one has sufficient time to accomplish all tasks on the agenda. In the event that you become aware of a potential inability to allocate sufficient time for accomplishing tasks, please promptly inform an appropriate individual. Inform them that it is infeasible for you to accomplish the task and provide a valid justification. Please do not harbor negative feelings towards this matter.

Your personal time and well-being are also of significance, and individuals who truly care will exhibit understanding. If rescheduling the task is not feasible, it is advisable to request that they assign the responsibility to another individual. It might require a considerable amount of time, but eventually you will acquire proficiency, leading to a higher level of ease. Please proceed at your own pace, ensuring that it aligns with your needs and objectives.

Strategy 6: Selective Ignorance

Effective leaders possess the ability to discern between matters of urgency and matters of importance. Frequently, that which holds significance to an individual is seldom accompanied by a sense of urgency. Pressing matters require your prompt consideration, though they may not necessarily constitute the foremost priority that warrants your focus.

Enlighten yourself about this distinction, and you will pave the way for a highly fruitful existence.

The key takeaway from this situation is to concentrate solely on matters that hold genuine significance to you.

Disregard matters of insignificance and triviality. Disregard individuals, occasions, and undertakings that divert your attention from what holds true significance to you.

The time has come to implement the concept of selective unawareness. Selective disregard refers to the judicious act of procrastination.

Put simply, abstain from reacting to every unforeseen event.

Allow others to handle the matter at hand.

Please refrain from interrupting unless it becomes absolutely necessary to address the circumstances. As the individual in a position of leadership/ownership, it is often enticing to personally address every concern. I comprehend and empathize with the emotions you are experiencing. Consider it as the establishment of a timeless brand image. Please be aware that your company's survival should not be solely dependent on the prevailing materialistic conditions of our world. Recruit individuals of exceptional caliber, place confidence in their abilities, and exercise prudent delay when necessary.

When Should you Procrastinate?

1. If you are aware of your team members' or managers' ability to effectively address the issue, it is advisable to refrain from involving yourself in the matter. It is crucial to have a thorough understanding of your pivotal responsibility and refrain from involvement in the issue.

2. If the attainment of optimal business outcomes relies on making sound decisions, it is imperative to pause and contemplate one's choices. This is not an opportune moment for hasty and ill-informed decision-making. Inhale deeply and deliberate upon this matter.

3. If the timing is inappropriate, refrain from executing the task. It is possible

that you are marketing a product that is influenced by seasonal fluctuations, and the current timing may not align with the market's demand.

Section 1: Before Work

What strategies can be implemented to effectively streamline your morning routine, thereby optimizing time management and productivity before commencing the work day?

The foremost action you can take is to execute duties and acquire necessary sustenance expeditiously in the morning, during a time when the stores are devoid of customers.

This task is not as challenging as it may initially appear. I would suggest waking up a bit earlier than usual and promptly commencing with your duties.

Efficiency Enhancement #1: Undertaking Errands during the Early Morning Hours

Alternative: Should you have the flexibility to commence your work at a later hour on a designated day of each week, it would be advisable not to disregard this opportunity. Acquire your customary food items instead.

This indicates that you will not be required to endure prolonged queues in order to inspect. You will not be required to expend as much effort in attempting to locate a parking space or navigating through traffic. This is especially remarkable for 24-hour supermarkets, as you can avail yourself of the opportunity to rise at 6 AM when the majority of individuals will not be present.

Familiarize yourself with the operating hours of your local grocery store. Previously, during my visits to the supermarket, I encountered the inconvenience of it being closed, requiring me to remain in close proximity.

Please inquire at nearby grocery stores. Determine the operating hours of the establishment, its opening time, and identify any nearby stores that operate round the clock. Efficiently complete assignments and acquire essential sustenance early in the morning, when those establishments are unoccupied.

This is a method through which you can substantially amplify your daily time savings. Suppose, for instance, that you limit your visits to the grocery store to once per week, resulting in a time savings of approximately 7 to 15 minutes that would otherwise have been consumed by queuing or searching for parking. Assuming that you manage to save approximately 10 minutes per day by following this approach. That totals approximately one minute per day.

How to Achieve High Productivity Despite Time Constraints

For several years, I made the conscious effort to acknowledge that if I were to possess an ample amount of free time, I would be able to accomplish significantly more. If I were to resign from my current employment and finish my education, I would have no concerns or obligations hindering me from managing my online business successfully. This would enable me to effortlessly introduce a new product every day and regularly produce ten articles. Regrettably, that assumption is significantly misplaced.

If one is engaging in a recreational pursuit or striving to develop a business concurrently with a regular profession or academic pursuits, it is possible to accomplish these aims by effectively managing one's time. The most favorable course of action would be to allocate sufficient time and channel it towards a constructive purpose: convince yourself that there is only one hour available to make progress in your business prior to attending to this particular task. I only have a one-hour window available for my scheduled lunch break.

One alternative way to convey the same message in a formal tone could be: "I am highly motivated to promptly finish my academic obligations, enabling me to subsequently initiate my entrepreneurial pursuits."

When you prioritize working smarter instead of investing more time or effort, you will experience a significant increase in efficiency. Could you possibly move several hours ahead of the planned schedule, and rise a few hours earlier and work without any disruptions? Is it accurate to assert that you will abstain from watching television, primarily on weekdays? Could you kindly limit your public engagement to just one evening per week?

I initiated my involvement with my online commerce venture at the age of 15, gained autonomy in my professional pursuits by 16, and successfully developed my inaugural product by the age of 17. I successfully finished my secondary education and managed to attend school while working full-time. It is possible!

During my academic tenure, I consistently strived to complete tasks assigned to me on the very day they were allocated, if feasible, irrespective of their deadlines being weeks ahead. I engaged in academic tasks while commuting, during the lunch break, and after school hours, recognizing the heightened potential for entrepreneurial endeavors as an independent operator. I observed a substantial increase in activity levels as I concluded my duties at the educational institution... With this intention, I would diligently finalize all academic tasks within the premises of the school library, refraining from any further academic considerations upon returning home.

During my previous employment, I proactively dedicated time to engage in various activities such as crafting items, composing articles and blog posts, and promoting to my list. Throughout my midday recess, during the 15-minute breaks, within work hours, and over the weekends.

You may require "greater opportunity" to complete your tasks; however, even if you had additional free time and devoted your entire life to your business, you would experience unhappiness and lack of motivation. Under circumstances where conditions are equitable, make use of that time continuum to maintain a high level of concentration on completing your obligations and making provision for additional ones.

The Mystery of Multi-Tasking

I am deeply disconcerted by the continued insistence of certain job recruiters on the inclusion of multi-tasking skills as a requirement for candidates. I have a genuine apprehension regarding the extent to which those companies prioritize the efficacy of their staff as opposed to the mere level of their busyness. Engaging in multiple tasks simultaneously can create an illusion of busyness, although it may not result in substantial productivity.

Engaging in multiple tasks simultaneously is the primary impediment to optimal productivity and effective time management. If you possess any reservations regarding the veracity of my statements, I encourage you to test the validity by engaging in the suggested action. Enlist the assistance of a companion to repeatedly toss 20 tennis balls to you in a continuous manner. It is imperative to successfully intercept all incoming balls while simultaneously engaging in the task of meticulously transcribing ten sentences onto a sheet of paper. Please document the duration required to complete both tasks. Afterwards, please proceed to reperform the two tasks individually, sequentially documenting the duration of each task. Observe and assess your emotions and the outcomes.

Why do people multi-task?

Due to the perception that we appear occupied when engaging in multiple tasks simultaneously. When we appear occupied, we tend to perceive ourselves as engaging in productive activities. This is so wrong. When engaged in multitasking, one repeatedly transitions between various tasks. Transitioning between tasks incurs a time cost; the more frequent the transitions, the greater the amount of time that is squandered.

What are the benefits or advantages of engaging in multitasking?

One ultimately consumes a greater amount of time when endeavoring to accomplish each individual task. Evidently, the act of shifting between tasks invariably results in a depletion of time, necessitating the allocation of additional time for each individual task.

You become less effective. Each time you transition to a different task, it will invariably require a certain amount of time to achieve a state of optimal focus and productivity. On occasion, one may enter a focused state wherein it becomes necessary to transition to a different task. In such instances, it is imperative to recommence the process of becoming fully engrossed in order to effectively engage with the new task. Upon returning to the previous task, it will be necessary to allocate sufficient time to readjust and regain focus in order to make up for any lost progress. Consequently, the overall caliber of your work will diminish.

You will experience heightened levels of stress. This outcome is a confluence of the preceding two outcomes. When one observes an increase in the duration required to accomplish tasks coupled with a decline in their quality, a sense of stress will likely arise.

Although there are certainly additional factors to consider when addressing productivity, it is important to recognize that multitasking serves as the primary impediment. I cannot overstate the significance of refraining from multitasking. It is recommended that you undertake the aforementioned assessment in order to observe an immediate boost in productivity upon discontinuing the practice of multitasking.

www.ingramcontent.com/pod-product-compliance
Lightning Source LLC
Chambersburg PA
CBHW050028130526
44590CB00042B/2052